HOOTER

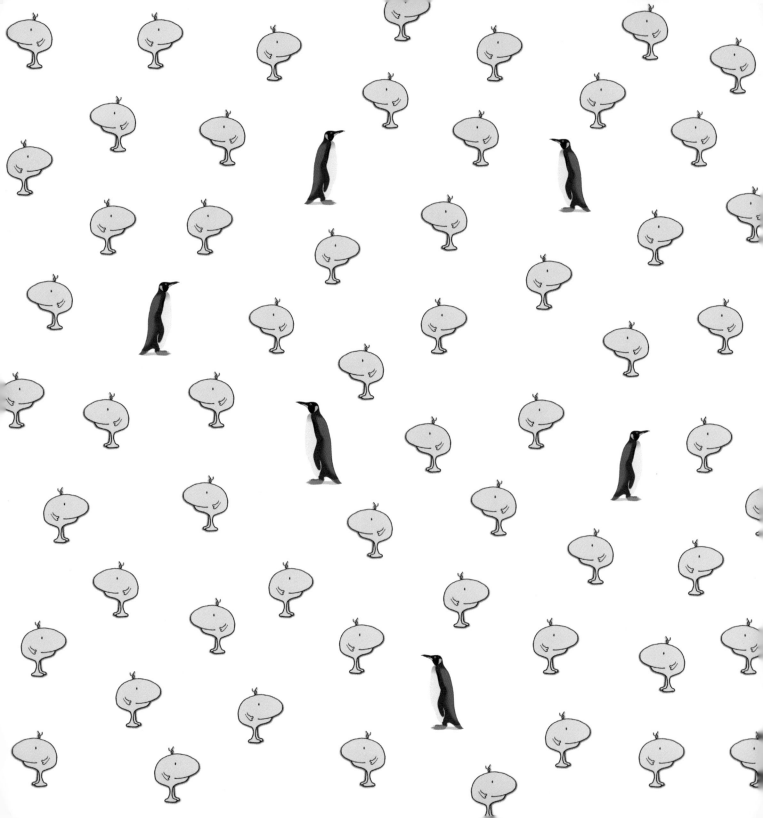

A Hooter Rhyming Picture Book

by Biro Jones

Original concept by Andrew Donaldson

Written and designed by Andrew Donaldson & Penny Pearson

Thank you!

HOOTER

at the Zoo

by Biro Jones

Hello Hooter, at the zoo,

Tell me what you see?

It's eating a banana,

And it's swinging in a tree.

It's a...

Monkey

Chewing leaves from tree tops,

Its legs and neck so tall.

Standing here beside it,

I feel so very small.

Giraffe

Feathers brightly colored,

Yellow, red and blue.

Take the time to stop and talk,

It says hello to you.

It's a...

Parrot

Lurking in the water,

What a toothy grin!

Careful of its jaws that snap,

Hooter don't fall in.

Crocodile

Giant tusks, ears that flap,

A trumpet for a nose.

Squirting water on its back,

Like a garden hose.

It's an...

Elephant

Orange body, smart black stripes,

Whiskers, giant paws.

Purring when it's happy,

When it's angry then it roars.

It's a...

Tiger

What a grumpy creature!

Watch it chomp and chew.

Sometimes it has one hump,

Sometimes it has two.

It's a...

Camel

Old and wise, plod, plod, plod,

Living in a shell.

What's that creature over there?

Hooter can you tell?

It's a...

Tortoise

Funny waddling on the rocks,

Bobbing left and right.

In the water chasing fish,

Feathers black and white.

It's a...

Penguin

Is this creature black and white?

Or is it white and black?

It looks a little like a horse,

With stripes all down its back.

Zebra

Watch it slither, watch it slide,

Watch it glide and hiss.

Scaly body, flicking tongue,

Hooter what is this?

Snake

Big fat bottom in the mud,

Yawning mouth so wide.

Hooter, please don't go too close,

You might fall inside.

It's a...

Hippo

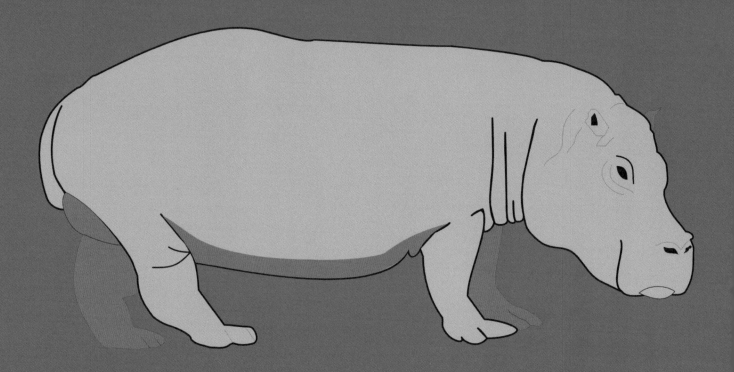

What a busy day at the zoo.

Bye-Bye Hooter. See you soon!

THANK YOU!

If you've enjoyed this book, Hooter would love you to leave a review. For more books, including our special offers, please visit the Biro Jones Amazon page.

www.amazon.com/author/birojones

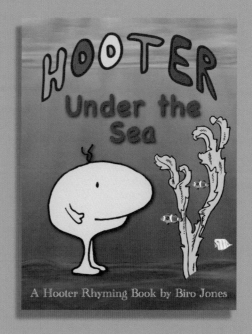

32832443R00021

Printed in Poland
by Amazon Fulfillment
Poland Sp. z o.o., Wrocław